Can I Really Know the Holy Spirit?

Anne Simpson

New Wine Press

New Wine Press
PO Box 17
Chichester
West Sussex PO20 6YB
England

ISBN: 1 874367 75 2

Typeset by CRB Associates, Reepham, Norfolk
Printed in England by Clays Ltd, St Ives plc.

Contents

	Acknowledgements	4
	Foreword	5
	Introduction	6
Chapter 1	Who is the Holy Spirit?	9
Chapter 2	Can I Really Know You?	17
Chapter 3	The Key to the Power	23
Chapter 4	Your Ministry Partner	36
Chapter 5	What Difference Will Knowing the Holy Spirit Make?	54

Acknowledgements

To my Mum and Dad
Many thanks for all your love, support and encouragement over the years, and for making this book possible.

To Suzanne
Many thanks for your work in typing and producing this manuscript for me.

If you are blessed by this book and would like to give a prayer request or receive further information about the ministry please write to me at:

Anne Simpson
Jesus Is Alive Ministries
PO Box 180
IPSWICH
IP1 2QF

Foreword

In this immensely practical book, Anne Simpson shows how any Christian, no matter how long they have been a Christian, whether for a few weeks or many years, can move from stagnation to growth, and know the person of the Holy Spirit in a personal way.

Using challenging questions, inspiring examples and clear biblical teaching, she urges each believer to seek to grow closer in their relationship with the Holy Spirit. To identify the barriers, and boldly step out into a new powerful way in their walk with God and the ministry he has given them.

Excellent teaching, sound advice and prime examples of how to live it.

Rev. Jimmy James

Introduction

This book has come about as a result of my search for a deeper relationship with God, and a longing to see the power of God in my own life and ministry.

If you are completely satisfied with your Christian life then this book is not for you. However if you have longed for a deeper relationship with God, if you have searched for the key to seeing the power of God manifest in your life, then I believe that this book will hold some of the answers that you have been looking for.

As you read this book, I pray that you will encounter the presence of the Holy Spirit, that he will reveal himself to you, and that you will come to know him as your friend. You may ask – 'Can I really know the Holy Spirit? I never realised it was possible to actually know the Holy Spirit.' The answer is 'Yes', the Holy Spirit longs to be your friend, and I pray that as you read this book you will find this wonderful reality for yourself and that your life will never be the same again.

Often when we think about the Holy Spirit we just think about the power and the miracles, and yet that is not the Holy Spirit. The miracles are just a part of what he does, but the Holy Spirit as a person is much more than miracles. It is like looking at a nurse or a bank manager and only seeing their job while not knowing anything about who they are, what emotions they have, what they like and dislike etc. You might know what they do but you know nothing about them as a person. When we first look at someone's job it is very easy to misunderstand who they are. We may look at a bank manager and assume that because he has a good job, that he is an upper-class person; we may even imagine what his life-style is like or what hobbies he does on the week-end. We may then look at someone who is a dustman and assume certain things about his personality. The danger in this is that we can be extremely wrong about someone when we judge them only by their job and outward appearance, and we don't know them as a person. The same is true of many Christians concerning the Holy Spirit. They know his job but they don't know him as a person. This can lead to people misunderstanding who the Holy Spirit really is.

Many people make two main mistakes when it comes to the Holy Spirit – they either ignore him or they call him 'it'. I often wonder how we would feel and react if we were treated in such a way. Just imagine for a moment that you attended a meeting and everybody ignored you, and every time you tried to speak you were brushed aside as if you were invisible. Would you be inclined to go back to that meeting again? I doubt it. You would feel hurt and rejected, and your response would probably be that next time you would go somewhere where you felt welcomed.

Do you realise that this is exactly what happens with the Holy Spirit? There are some churches where he has withdrawn his presence because he has been ignored. We need to understand that the Holy Spirit is a gentleman and never enters where he is not welcome. How sad to think that by our ignorance we could turn away from our midst the most wonderful person we could ever meet.

Our second mistake is to call him 'it'. We acknowledge his presence but not his person. Again imagine you went to a meeting and this time people did speak to you, but they kept calling you 'it'. Think how you would feel if the Minister of the church pointed to you and said 'it will now come and pray for us'. Would you feel like praying for the people in a nice manner? Yet how do we think the Holy Spirit feels when we call upon him for miracles and power, and yet we can't even address him properly. No wonder we often lack the power that we long to see. We have grieved the Holy Spirit.

Jesus said (John 16:7):

'Unless I go away, the Counsellor will not come to you, but if I go I will send him to you.'

Jesus was telling his disciples that he would soon leave them to ascend back to his Father but he wouldn't leave them alone, he would send someone else to be with them. Jesus called him a Counsellor – the Holy Spirit.

A Counsellor is one who comes alongside and listens to us, and we speak to someone who is a Counsellor. The Holy Spirit longs for an intimate relationship with us. Now you may ask:

– Do we pray to the Holy Spirit?
– Do we worship the Holy Spirit?

No, we fellowship with the Holy Spirit and he helps us to pray and always leads us to worship Jesus. To fellowship with someone means spending time with them, talking with them. In 2 Corinthians 13:14 we read:

'May the grace of the Lord Jesus Christ, and the love of God, and the fellowship of the Holy Spirit be with you all.'

I want to share with you through this book about the person of the Holy Spirit and how you can come to know him as your friend and ministry partner.

The word used here for fellowship is *'koinonia'* which literally means 'a joining/sharing, a partnership'. The relationship with the Holy Spirit should be one of a joining and sharing together in every way.

Chapter 1

Who is the Holy Spirit?

The Holy Spirit is God! He is the third Person of the Trinity, but not third in position. He is equal to the Father and the Son and yet he has his own unique personality. In Ephesians 4:30 we read, *'Do not grieve the Holy Spirit'* indicating that he is the most sensitive member of the Godhead. He is easily offended and he will withdraw from wherever he is not welcome.

We need to also understand that the Holy Spirit has always been God. He didn't just suddenly arrive on the day of Pentecost any more than Jesus didn't just suddenly appear at Bethlehem. In John 1 we read:

> *'In the beginning was the Word, and the Word was with God, and the Word was God.'*

Here we see that Jesus who is the Word made flesh was not only with God the Father in the beginning, but he was God. In the same way the Holy Spirit has always been God. In Genesis 1 we see that it was the Spirit of God that moved upon the waters. The Holy Spirit was involved in creation just as much as the Father and the Son were.

The Holy Spirit is the Spirit of God. In the same way that each of us has a spirit within us, so the Spirit inside God is The Holy Spirit.

> *'For who among men knows the thoughts of a man except the man's spirit within him? In the same way no-one knows the thoughts of God except the Spirit of God.'*
>
> (1 Corinthians 2:11–12)

The spirit within each of us is the real 'us'. As we look at the Holy Spirit and hear his voice, what we are seeing and hearing is the very heart of God.

What Does the Holy Spirit Do?

He glorifies Jesus

'He will bring glory to me.'   (John 16:14)

The first and foremost job of the Holy Spirit is to bring glory to
Jesus. Often people get worried about what will happen if they
start speaking to the Holy Spirit – will Jesus get neglected? This
can never be the case because whenever we speak to the Holy
Spirit, his main job is to reveal more of Jesus to us. He makes
Jesus real. That's why in a meeting where the Holy Spirit
is present people get healed, as I'll share later, because he is
making Jesus real and whenever Jesus is made real, people will
be healed. In the gospels, any time someone touched Jesus
they were healed.

He convicts of sin

'He will convict the world of guilt.'   (John 16:8)

The Holy Spirit is the one who will convict people of their
sin and their need of Jesus. Have you ever done something
wrong and then felt a niggling feeling? The Holy Spirit is our
conscience, he does not bring condemnation but he does bring
conviction. Condemnation pulls us down and offers no
answer, but conviction points us to a different way.

He teaches and reminds

'The Holy Spirit whom the Father will send in my name, will teach
you all things and will remind you of everything I have said to
you.'   (John 14:26)

It is the Holy Spirit who helps us to understand the Word of
God. He helps us to make sense of what we have read. He is also
the one who will bring back to our memory a certain passage of
scripture at the correct time. We may find ourselves one day in
a situation where we don't know what to do and suddenly an
appropriate verse will come into our heart and mind. This I
believe is the Holy Spirit reminding us of the Word of God for
our particular situation.

He will speak guidance to us

The cloud

In the Old Testament we see that the cloud was a symbol of the Holy Spirit. God used the cloud to guide the Israelites in the wilderness, and they would only move when the cloud moved. Whenever the cloud did not move, they remained in the camp.

The cloud was also a symbol of the glory of God. Whenever the priests entered into the holy of holies, a cloud would descend. When Moses set up the tabernacle, the cloud descended. When Solomon built the Temple, the cloud descended. The cloud symbolised the presence of God.

The Israelites were totally dependent upon the cloud for their every movement.

> *'Whenever the cloud lifted from above the tabernacle, they would set out; but if the cloud did not lift, they did not set out.'*
>
> (Exodus 40:36)

Whenever Moses would go to the Tent of Meeting to speak with the Lord, a cloud would descend at the entrance of the tent while Moses spoke with the Lord.

> *'The law is only a shadow of the good things that are coming – not the realities themselves.'* (Hebrews 10:1)

You see, they followed a cloud but not a person, they followed a symbol of the power of God but we have the real person living within us. They could only look from a distance and see a strange mist, but we can have an intimate relationship with a real person, not with a cloud.

> *'When he, the Spirit of truth, comes, he will guide you into all truth. He will not speak on his own; he will speak only what he hears, and he will tell you what is yet to come.'* (John 16:13)

It is the Holy Spirit who will speak to us and tell us the will of the Father. He is one with the Father and Jesus, and the Bible says that he will not speak his own separate will, but he will only tell you what he is told to tell you. The passage states that he will tell us what is yet to come. I believe that this can be in the form of visions concerning things that are planned for us in the future, or warnings about situations which are not good for us.

'I only know that in every city the Holy Spirit warns me that prison and hardships are facing me.'   (Acts 20:23)

Paul was warned by the Holy Spirit of what was ahead, but notice something interesting: Paul said *'compelled by the Spirit I am going to Jerusalem'* (Acts 20:22).

It was the Holy Spirit who compelled him to go and at the same time warned him of the dangers. Here we see that some things that God asks us to do may not always be easy, but Paul had a choice whether to go or not, and his response was:

'I consider my life worth nothing to me, if only I may finish the race and complete the task the Lord Jesus has given me – the task of testifying to the gospel of God's grace.'   (Acts 20:24)

He knew the dangers ahead and yet his greatest desire was to fulfil the call of God upon his life and to finish the race, because he was looking to a greater reward in heaven.

'I will pour out my Spirit on all people. Your sons and daughters will prophesy.'   (Joel 2:28)

Here we see an example of how the Holy Spirit will tell us things yet to come through other Christians. The Holy Spirit speaks to us either directly on a one to one basis, or he can choose to use another Christian to bring a word of prophecy to us. As with any of the Gifts it is important that we test all that is given to us. We should not accept everything as being 'God hath spoken' nor should we reject something without checking it first.

'Do not treat prophecies with contempt, test everything, hold on to the good.'   (1 Thessalonians 5:20)

If a prophecy does not match the Word of God then it needs to be rejected.

He chooses people for ministry

'While they were worshipping the Lord and fasting, the Holy Spirit said "set apart for me Barnabas and Saul for the work to which I have called them."'   (Acts 13:2)

Notice something here; it was while they were worshipping and fasting that the Holy Spirit spoke and gave guidance and calling. If we are seeking a call of God upon our lives, we too need to worship and fast in order to hear the voice of the Holy Spirit more clearly.

Are you seeking to be used more by God? Do you want to know the ministry God has for you? It is the Holy Spirit who chooses people for ministry, so you need to get to know him.

Speaking from a natural point of view, in my ministry team I would much prefer to have people on my team who I know and get on well with, rather than people with enormous talent that I don't get on with! Why? Because unity is more powerful than talents. Because if you have a united team with one heart and one mind, then God will give the anointing, the equipping and the talents. We are only the vessels anyway and he is the filler of the vessels. What does that have to do with the Holy Spirit choosing people for ministry you may ask? The answer is, quite a lot, because in the same way as I would choose people I know well for my earthly team, how much more will the Holy Spirit choose people he knows well for his heavenly team! I believe that the Holy Spirit searches throughout the earth for men and women to be on his team, and when he searches he doesn't look for talent, strength, charisma, status etc. He simply looks for a willing heart who is willing to yield to him. I want to work with people I know and so does the Holy Spirit. If you know someone, communication is easier. If we know the Holy Spirit it will be easier for him to lead and direct us in the ministry.

> *'The Lord has sought out a man after his own heart and appointed him leader of the people.'*   (1 Samuel 13:14)

> *'He will do everything I want him to do.'*   (Acts 13:22)

The Lord sought out David; that means that God didn't just say 'oh, you'll do, but he earnestly looked until he found the right person for the job, and it was not the person that others would have chosen. David was just a young shepherd boy, not even considered by his family and yet God chose him because he saw his heart. Maybe you feel today that you don't have much to offer God, but the question is, are you prepared to give God a willing heart? You see God chose Moses to bring deliverance to the Israelites and yet Moses said:

> *'Who am I that I should go?'*   (Exodus 3:11)

God didn't make any reply as to who Moses was but he simply said:

> *'I will be with you.'*   (Exodus 3:12)

In other words if God is with us, it doesn't matter who or what we are. It is his ability within us that matters. Moses however was still not convinced and so God says:

> *' "What is that in your hand?" "A staff," he replied.'*
>   (Exodus 4:2)

> *'Take this staff in your hand, so that you can perform miraculous signs with it.'*   (Exodus 4:17)

God was saying to Moses 'What do you have?' – 'Oh Lord not much, just a stick,' but you see, a rotten old stick given into the hands of Jesus can perform miracles. Whatever you have, however small, if you give it to Jesus he will perform miracles with it. Today – what do you have? 'Not much Lord, just a rotten broken life with a willing heart.' Jesus will take that willing heart and perform miracles with it and he'll mend the rest of your life at the same time. Isn't that wonderful!

The Lord takes the weak and the foolish to confound the wise. Now in Judges 6 God comes to Gideon

> *'The Lord is with you, mighty warrior.'*   (Judges 6:12)

God saw Gideon as a mighty warrior, but that wasn't how he saw himself.

> *'My clan is the weakest, I am the least.'*   (Judges 6:15)

He didn't see himself as being capable of the task that God was calling him to, but notice what God says in verse 16 – *'I will be with you.'* Today he speaks the same words to you that he spoke to Moses.

You may say:

– 'Who am I that I should go?'
– 'I have never been eloquent in speech,'
– 'Someone else would do a better job,'
– 'I am the weakest and the least,'

and God answers all your excuses and fears in one sentence 'I will be with you.' When God says 'I will be with you,' every argument disappears, because if God is there nothing else matters.

It is the Holy Spirit who chooses people for ministry and it is also the Holy Spirit who equips people for ministry.

He equips and empowers us

God never tells us to do something without giving us the ability to do it. In 1 Corinthians 12 we read of all of the Gifts of the Spirit.

> *'All these are the work of the one spirit and he gives them to each one just as he determines.'*　　(1 Corinthians 12:11)

So we see it is the Holy Spirit who chooses who to give the gifts to. Later in the book we will look at these gifts and how they help us to witness for Jesus.

> *'You will receive power when the Holy Spirit comes upon you and you will be my witnesses.'*　　(Acts 1:8)

It is the Holy Spirit who chooses people for ministry, it is the Holy Spirit who distributes the gifts needed for the job and it is the Holy Spirit who empowers us for the job. Even Jesus himself was dependent upon the Holy Spirit while he was on earth, and we need to be too.

He counsels us

> *'Unless I go the Counsellor will not come.'*　　(John 16:7)

Jesus referred to the Holy Spirit as a Counsellor. I believe that each and every one of us needs someone to talk to, someone who will listen to us and not judge us, someone who will understand the way that we feel. The sad truth is that so many people are more interested in talking than listening. However there is one person we can talk to who will listen and understand, and he is 'the Counsellor, the Holy Spirit.'

The Holy Spirit understands everything about you and he will listen and comfort you. Not only will he listen and comfort you but he will advise you what to do in your situation. We can go to many different people and be given lots of different advice, but the Holy Spirit will give you the wisdom of God. Another wonderful fact is that the Holy Spirit doesn't gossip! Too often we go to a person who we think we can trust, and we share our most personal problem with them, only to find that the very next week half the church knows all about our personal problem. This is not the case with the Holy Spirit. He is very discreet and anything that you share with him will go no further than the throne-room of God.

> *'No-one knows the thoughts of God, except the Spirit of God.'*
> (1 Corinthians 2:11)

– Do you want to know the will of God for your situation?
– Do you want to know what you should do?

The Holy Spirit knows the answers. Why don't you ask him to share them with you?

He helps us to pray

> *'We do not know what we ought to pray for but the Spirit himself intercedes for us.'*   (Romans 8:26)

We will look at this in more detail in the chapter 'What Difference Will the Holy Spirit Make?', but we see that he is the one who will help us to pray. If we were left to our own devices we would not have a clue how to pray. Even the disciples who had spent a lot of time with Jesus, still said:

> *'Lord, teach us to pray.'*

Today it is the Holy Spirit who will teach us to pray.

Chapter 2

Can I Really Know You?

Knowing the Holy Spirit is much more than speaking in tongues or even moving in the other gifts of the Spirit. Often when we speak in tongues we think that we have arrived and that we know everything there is to know about the Holy Spirit. If I came to your door and gave you a gift, the gift is only what I give, it is not me. The giver of the gifts wants to know us.

There were many times when I said 'Holy Spirit, can I really know you? I would like to meet you; can we be friends?' The Holy Spirit responded by not only revealing his presence, but his person. Often we may be in a meeting and we can sense the presence of the Holy Spirit but he wants to know you even closer than just his presence. He wants you to talk to him and share with him. He wants to hold you in his arms and comfort you. You may say 'Anne, I have never thought of the Holy Spirit in such a way.' Maybe one of the reasons that we find it so hard to think of the Holy Spirit as a person is because we can't imagine what he looks like. We tend to think of him as wind or a dove, rather than a person. We often think of him as a wind, we associate him as just a power, a presence we feel rather than a person. After all you may say, how can we have a relationship with the wind or a dove? Yet these are just symbols used to describe him, in the same way as Jesus is referred to as a lamb or a lion, and yet we do not really think of him as looking like a lamb, they are just symbolic. You may now say 'well, what does the Holy Spirit look like then?'

I believe that the Holy Spirit looks very much like Jesus. As I was preparing to preach at a meeting one day about the Holy Spirit, the Lord gave me a picture. I imagined that I was standing in the hall and that a man with a long white robe was standing next to me. I couldn't see his face but just this long flowing robe and his hands stretched out. As I began to preach I saw him move out into the congregation and begin to lay hands on the people. I believe I saw a picture of the Holy Spirit.

There have been several times since then when I have been praying and speaking to the Holy Spirit, that as I close my eyes I see a person with the same long flowing robe standing in front of me. I will share with you in a later chapter about how knowing the person of the Holy Spirit will transform your ministry as well as your life. When we speak, whether it be on a one to one basis or to a crowd, the Holy Spirit will transform your normal words into something dynamic. He will take away from you all your strivings and frustration and you will flow.

Earlier we looked at how he is often thought of as a wind. Imagine the wind for a minute; have you ever been walking along the beach on a windy day? Sometimes, especially in East Anglia, the wind can be so strong it nearly lifts you off your feet. The wind is powerful. When the wind is that powerful, it is much easier to walk in the same direction as the wind and let it blow you along than it is to try to walk against it. The same is true of the Holy Spirit, we need to walk in the same direction as he is moving, to allow ourselves to be blown along, rather than trying to walk against the Spirit.

Maybe the reason we resist the Holy Spirit is because we are afraid where he may take us; it may not be where we had intended to go. We can sometimes be a people who want to be in control of what is going to happen in our lives. The truth though, friends, is that when we are in control of our lives we usually make a mess of things and end up crying out to God. So why not save yourselves a lot of heartache and let him take control in the first place, because he knows you better than you know yourself, and he will only lead you to places that are in the centre of the will of God.

> *'They that wait upon the Lord shall renew their strength, they shall mount up with wings as eagles.'*   (Isaiah 40:31)

An eagle does not flap its wings like most birds, he just glides on the wind. We can see here a picture of how God intends us to live. He doesn't want us to get in a flap! He doesn't want us to have to strive all the time to make things happen. He wants us to flow in the Spirit.

As we allow the wind of the Holy Spirit to take us up, we glide wherever he wants to take us. Maybe this is what Paul had in mind when he spoke of walking by the Spirit – just letting him take us wherever he wants. It's not so much following the Holy Spirit as allowing him to take control of us. The Lord wants us to soar up higher than we have ever been before into a new dimension. The Holy Spirit will take you up into a higher level of the presence of God. Have you noticed that during a time of praise and worship certain songs seem to bring the anointing of God into a meeting? But then someone can come in and sing something completely out of line with the way the Spirit is moving, and it can cut right through the presence. You feel yourself doing a nose-dive back down. Was this what Jesus referred to when he spoke about worshipping in Spirit and in Truth (John 4:24)?

At some of our Missions recently I have experienced this happening. During the worship sometimes there was such an awesome sense of the presence of God, that we hardly dared say the wrong thing and break the anointing. We have found that some songs do seem to bring the anointing of God, I don't know why, but they just do.

Sometimes the anointing can be so tangible that you can almost reach out your hand and touch Jesus.

Philippians 3:3 says *'We who worship by the Spirit of God.'* We need to be sensitive in our worship to how the Holy Spirit is moving. We can never predict or presume how the Holy Spirit will move. This is why we need to get rid of our traditions and be open to his leading. The Holy Spirit cannot move in a place where we stick religiously to the pattern we have had for years. Knowing the Holy Spirit is so exciting, because you never know what is going to happen next. There have been many times when I have gone to a meeting with my notes prepared for a message, but either before I start or even half way through, the notes get thrown to one side because the Holy Spirit has changed the message. I find that sometimes these become some of the most exciting and anointed meetings as my response has been 'Well, Holy Spirit, you had better put some words in my mouth,' and he always does. As we come to a place where we are totally dependent on him, he never lets us down.

Do you realise that the Holy Spirit has always known you, even though you may not have known him? He has always been there, for the Bible says in Psalm 139:7:

'Where can I go from your Spirit?'

and in verse 13:

'For you created my inmost being, you knit me together in my mother's womb.'

Wow! Not only was the Holy Spirit involved in the creation of the world but he was involved in your creation. He saw your unformed body in your mother's womb; he knows everything about you. The Bible says in John 16:8 that *'the Holy Spirit will convict the world of guilt.'* Right from before you were born, the Holy Spirit was assigned to watch over you, and during your life to convict you and draw you to Jesus

Who do you think brought you to Jesus? You may say 'My friend told me about Jesus.' Well maybe they did, but who convicted you that what you were hearing was the truth? It was the one who wants to be your greatest friend – the Holy Spirit. He's always been there, and he was longing for you to come to Jesus, so that you could also know the Holy Spirit who all your life was drawing you to Jesus.

Jesus said in John 16:7:

'Unless I go away, the Counsellor will not come to you, but if I go I will send him to you.'

It would seem that the Holy Spirit could not come to the earth fully until Jesus had returned to the Father. Previously, throughout the Bible we just see the Holy Spirit coming upon certain people for certain tasks, but never remaining upon all believers. Jesus says to his disciples that he will soon be leaving them, but he'll send someone else to look after them and guide them. Jesus expected that they would get to know this person in the same way as they knew Jesus. The disciples had walked with Jesus, shared with him through good and bad times, eaten with him, ministered with him, but now he was leaving. The words that Jesus spoke, would indicate that he expected them to treat the Holy Spirit in the same way as they had treated him, and to have the same relationship with him as they had had with Jesus. No matter how much the disciples wanted him to stay, the fact was he was leaving and they had to get to know the Holy Spirit. Do you realise, that at no point after the day of Pentecost did the Holy Spirit ascend back to heaven like Jesus? He is still here on the earth as the one that Jesus sent to be with us. So often we cry out 'Oh God where are you? You seem so far away.' Maybe we've forgotten that the words Jesus spoke to his disciples, he also spoke for every believer. He has sent someone to be nearer to you than any human ever could be.

This day, I challenge you to say 'Holy Spirit I would like to know you. Can we be friends?' I guarantee that he will answer you. You may ask 'What will happen if I say that?' The answer to that is 'I don't know.' For some it may be a dramatic experience. You may fall shaking on your face and receive great visions from heaven. For others you may sense nothing much at all except a warm knowing deep inside that he has answered you, and that your relationship with him will gradually begin to grow from this day forward.

I have to admit that none of my Christian experiences to date have been big flashes in the sky. Although my conversion to Christ was dramatic in as much as where God brought me from, it was not an overnight experience. It was a gradual process of Jesus becoming real in my life. In the same way when I came to know the Holy Spirit, it was a gradual process of speaking with him daily and getting to know him. Each of us is different and God deals with each of us in a different way. Maybe for me the gradual process builds a stronger relationship than a dramatic experience that soon fades away.

Having said all this, the gradual process is by no means dull; everything about getting to know the Holy Spirit is dynamic and exciting. There are times when I am so excited that I cannot sleep at night. Sometimes I couldn't even tell you what I'm excited about, but I feel like a kid on Christmas Eve with an excitement and expectation of what is going to happen. I believe that on these occasions the Holy Spirit is witnessing to my spirit that there are exciting things about to happen.

Knowing the Holy Spirit will give you inspirations like you've never had before. The inspiration and ability to write this book is one. In my natural ability I could never do anything like this, but the Holy Spirit takes us out of our natural ability into supernatural ability. Sometimes I will be lying in bed, and the Holy Spirit starts to give me ideas for messages, and I have to get up and start writing them down before I forget them. At other times, I'll sit down to write a message, and the words from the Holy Spirit will come so quickly that the pen wants to move quicker than my hand! When you come to know the Holy Spirit he will take the dryness away from you. No longer will you sit for hours striving to write one word towards a message.

When we know and walk with the Holy Spirit we will just automatically be in the right place at the right time. There have been occasions where I have decided to go to a town to go shopping, thinking it's me that's decided to go. When I've got there, I have bumped into people that are able to help with a particular situation I needed help with at that time. I had not heard a loud booming voice saying '**Today** go to the Shopping Centre.' We often think that being led by the Spirit is hearing voices of direction all the time. Although the Lord does speak to us, a lot of the time things just fall into place because we are allowing the Holy Spirit to lead us anyway.

I challenge you today to let go of trying to control your own life and allow the Holy Spirit to take control.

Chapter 3

The Key to the Power

There were many times after meetings when I would go home, and cry out to God in frustration 'Lord, I want to see something happen.' I saw in the Bible a gospel of power and yet my experiences didn't seem to match that. I reasoned that God has not changed, and that if I didn't see the same power today, there had to be a reason – my experience needed to change to match the Word of God. We often tend to think that God has changed, when in fact our response should be that we are the ones who need to change. I decided to ask God, and to seek for the key to the same power as I saw in the Bible.

I remember someone praying for me to receive a new anointing and as they prayed, my cry to God was 'Lord I'm fed up with seeing a bit here and there. I want to see and move in the dynamic.' I believe that God responds to a hungry heart that is not satisfied until we receive and move in the fullness that he has for us. Too often we give up, concluding that it's not God's will to heal someone or set them free or it's not God's time for revival in the nation. Although I acknowledge the timings of God, we must not allow this to be an excuse for why things so often don't happen. We need to be a people who will not be satisfied until we move in what God has promised us. Instead of being surprised when someone is healed, we should get to the place where we are more surprised when they don't get healed than when they do, because Jesus said that when we lay hands on the sick they **will** get well (Mark 16:18).

In Acts 1:8 Jesus said to his disciples *'You shall receive power.'* How? When? *'When the Holy Spirit comes upon you.'* The key to the power, the source of the power is the Holy Spirit himself. He is the power of God.

The saying goes that if you spend long enough with someone

you will become like them. If we want the anointing power of
God in our lives then we need to rub shoulders with the Holy
Spirit and the anointing will rub off on us.

The Lord began to reveal to me that if I wanted to see the
miracles, the signs and wonders, then I needed to get to know
the Holy Spirit. Once I remember reading of how Peter's
shadow healed the sick and I fell on my knees and cried out
'Lord you are the same now as you were then. I want to see
these kind of things happening in my life.'

I began to see that even in the life of Jesus, he was totally
dependent upon the Holy Spirit. We do not read of him being
in any public ministry until the Holy Spirit had come upon
him. Up until then he had probably lived a very ordinary life,
much like you and I.

> *'Jesus was baptised too and as he was praying, heaven was opened*
> *and the Holy Spirit descended on him in bodily form like a dove . . .*
> *Now Jesus was about thirty years old when he began his ministry.'*
> (Luke 3:21, 23)

Jesus did not begin his ministry until the Holy Spirit had
come upon him. Then after this he was led into the desert to be
tempted by the Devil. It was only after he had overcome with
the Word of God that he was able to stand up and proclaim in
Luke 4:18 *'The Spirit of the Lord is upon me because he has
anointed me.'*

Here I believe we see a pattern to the receiving of the
anointing. If we want the anointing we must pray. It was only
as Jesus was praying that heaven opened. Then he had to go
through a testing time and overcome before he was released
into his ministry. Sometimes the Lord may take us through a
time of testing to see if we can be trusted with the anointing
before he will release us fully. Jesus could have given in to
receiving all the splendour that the Devil was offering him, but
he chose to worship the Father only, and because of this, the
Father gave him a greater splendour. When God gives us an
anointing we need to be careful that we don't claim the glory
for ourselves. Jesus remained dependent on the Holy Spirit all
the way through his ministry. In Luke 5:17 we read:

> *'The power of the Lord was present for him to heal the sick.'*

Who is the passage referring to? Jesus was ministering and the power was present for him to heal! It was the Holy Spirit who was present – if Jesus needed the presence of the Holy Spirit to heal the sick, how much more do we need him? Every time I go to minister at a meeting I say 'Holy Spirit I need you, if you're not there I'm not going,' because I know that I have nothing to offer the people, but the Holy Spirit has everything to offer.

So often we hear people speak about the Holy Spirit descending upon a meeting, or you'll hear people praying for the Holy Spirit to come down. I believe that the Holy Spirit has already come down once on the day of Pentecost, and he didn't go back up anywhere since. The Holy Spirit came to the earth, and is still working on the earth. I don't believe that the Holy Spirit comes down in a meeting but I believe he arrives in a meeting. Instead of praying for the Holy Spirit to come down, we need to be saying 'Holy Spirit we welcome you, you have an invitation to come to our meeting tonight' and if he's invited, he'll show up. How wonderful it is when the Holy Spirit arrives. He is the VIP guest and should be treated as such. When the Queen comes to an event, people line the streets with flags and roll out a red carpet. There is a sense of expectation in waiting for royalty to arrive. How much more should we put out the flags and the red carpet for the highest royalty of all. When the Holy Spirit comes to your meeting, make sure he is welcomed 100 times more than any earthly royalty would be.

I have begun to notice recently that people are beginning to get healed and set free just sitting in the meetings. I sometimes have not even laid hands on them or gone anywhere near them; it has just been the presence of the Holy Spirit in the meeting who has touched them. Recently people have come saying that while they were sitting in a meeting or during a time of worship, they felt a tremendous heat go through their body, and they were healed before I even gave a call for people to come for healing. This proves that the key to the power is not you or me but the presence of the Holy Spirit.

The Cost of the New Anointing

I believe that there is something called a 'New Anointing' which is coming upon men and women of God at this time. I believe that we are about to see the greatest move of God in this nation that has ever taken place. I believe that it will be a move of power with more signs and wonders than we've even seen before. Some time back, God began speaking to me about how he was going to shake this nation. I then saw a picture of a big dam about to burst and as it did so, the water flooded everywhere. I believe that the dam is the walls that have been built up against God in many different ways over the years, but as people have been praying for Revival, the dam is starting to burst. As it does there will be such a mighty outpouring of the Holy Spirit across this land, and anyone who tries to stand in the way will be swept away.

My desire was, 'Lord I want to be a part of what you're doing,' and I earnestly desired a greater anointing upon my life. One time I was crying to God for a 'New Anointing' and I sensed God saying to me 'if you really want it, it will cost you time – you need to come away with me by yourself.' As I went away to seek God for the New Anointing, I knew an hour before I was due to come home that I had received it, and God also spoke to me about being lifted to a higher level in him. I don't fully understand all of these things but I believe that we can ask God to take us to a higher level, a higher dimension in him. I believe that the higher level is not just in terms of 'the Power' but a higher level of relationship with God where he wants to reveal new and deeper revelations to us. If you desire to move to a higher level in God, then go by yourself to a quiet place, and ask God to take you there.

A Holy Spirit Encounter

'The disciples were together with the door locked for fear of the Jews.'   (John 20:19)

After Jesus had been arrested and crucified, the disciples were both disillusioned and afraid. We see here in John 20 that they were in fear of their own lives and they were keeping themselves hidden away for fear that they might be the next ones to be arrested. But then a few chapters later we see a dynamic transformation. In Acts 2 we see Peter standing up and proclaiming a message so boldly that 3,000 people got saved. Then in Acts 3 we read of how Peter and John were on their way to the temple when they came across a lame man sitting by the gate. Taking hold of his hand they said *'in the name of Jesus walk.'* Even after they were then arrested and warned not to speak any longer in the name of Jesus they replied *'we cannot help speaking about what we have seen and heard'* (Acts 4:20). They were no longer afraid, they had become bold. What had happened to change these men so dramatically from being afraid and hiding, to being bold and proclaiming? The answer lies in Acts 2:4:

'All of them were filled with the Holy Spirit,'

and Acts 4:31:

'They were all filled with the Holy Spirit and spoke the Word of God boldly.'

They had an **encounter with the Holy Spirit** and he changed their lives forever. If we then read through the book of Acts we see that miracles, signs and wonders were an everyday part of the apostles ministry.

*'When the crowds heard Philip and **saw** the miraculous signs he did, they all paid close attention to what he said.'* (Acts 8:6)

When the people saw the power, they listened to his words. We need an encounter with the Holy Spirit, so that people will see the power of God, and then listen to our words. Paul says in 1 Corinthians 2:4:

'My message and my preaching were not with wise and persuasive words, but with a demonstration of the Spirit's power.'

The Gospel is proclamation and demonstration. Jesus said that we are to expect signs to follow the preaching of the Word. The source of the power is the Holy Spirit.

'By the power of signs and miracles through the power of the Spirit.' (Romans 15:19)

If we want miracles to flow out of our lives then we need an encounter with the Holy Spirit.

In the Old Testament the Holy Spirit came upon certain people for certain tasks, but now he is readily available for all believers. Jesus said John 14:12:

'Anyone who has faith in me will do what I have been doing. He will do even greater things than these because I am going to the Father.'

Jesus was saying that any believer has the potential to do even greater things then he did! Then he tells us why – it is because he is going to the Father. You may wonder what relevance that has to us being able to do greater things. In John 16:7 Jesus said:

'It is good that I am going away, unless I go away the Counsellor will not come to you.'

It was only after Jesus had returned to the Father, that the Holy Spirit was allowed to come to the earth and to fill every believer who desires him.

'I am going to send you what my Father has promised, but stay in the city until you have been clothed with power from on high.'

(Luke 24:19)

God has given the potential for every believer to be filled with the fullness of the Holy Spirit, and to have daily fellowship with him. The source of all miracles dwells on the earth and in believers. If we realised what this really meant, I believe we could shake this world in Jesus' name. Do we truly understand what Jesus said when he said *'You shall be clothed with power'* (NIV), or *'You shall be endued with power'* (KJV). Let's look at these two words, 'clothed' and 'endued'.

Elijah's Mantle

In the Old Testament a mantle, or cloak was a symbol of the anointing. In 1 Kings 19 we read of Elijah going to Elisha and *'Elijah went up to him and threw his cloak around him'* (verse 19). Elijah was throwing his anointing onto Elisha to succeed him as prophet. In verse 21 we read that *'he set out to become his attendant.'* After Elisha had received the call and the anointing, he needed to be in a time of training, and he ministered under Elijah. I believe that the first step to receiving a New Anointing is to have a servant heart and be faithful in another person's ministry. So many people believe that they have a call to preach and yet they are not prepared to serve. Jesus, although he was God himself, came to serve others. As we are faithful with small things, God will give us greater responsibilities. When the time came for Elijah to be taken up to heaven, he asked Elisha what he wanted, and Elisha replied *'Let me inherit a double portion of your Spirit'* (2 Kings 2:9).

Sometimes we can receive an anointing and think that is all that is available, and yet Elisha wanted more than what he already had. I believe that the second step to receiving the anointing is a hungry heart, a heart that desires the anointing. God responds to a hungry heart. We will never receive the anointing by saying 'Well, if God gives it to me then it will just happen.' Anything that we receive from God has to be desired earnestly.

Elisha could have stayed where he was, but he refused to stay put, he wanted to move on. Three times Elijah said to Elisha – *'stay here, the Lord has sent me somewhere else,'* but Elisha refused to stay where he was. We can be comfortable in our church routine and happy with all that we have experienced, or we can say 'I know there is far more, and I'm moving on.' Elijah replies *'You have asked a difficult thing'* (2 Kings 2:10). Why had he asked a difficult thing?

Often we tend to think only of the glamour of the anointing and not the cost. We want the miracles, the signs and wonders, but do we want to spend long times in prayer? Do we want to fast when we don't feel like it? Are we prepared to put up with criticism and opposition? If you look at the life of any anointed person you will see a great deal of sacrifice behind the scenes. Elijah knew the cost of what Elisha was asking for, he knew it would not be easy. Elijah knew of the mountain-top victories with the prophets of Baal, but he also knew of the loneliness he felt in the cave when his life was threatened.

Also, the greater the anointing, the greater the responsibility and accountability there is to God.

> *'From the one who has been entrusted with much, much more will be asked.'* (Luke 12:48)

If God gives us an anointing, one day he will want to know what we did with it. The greater the anointing, the greater our responsibility. Elijah knew that it would not be easy for Elisha, so he said *'You have asked a difficult thing, yet if you see me when I am taken, it will be yours – otherwise not.'*

Why was this the case? The answer I believe, is because if we want the anointing of the Holy Spirit, we have to look heavenwards. Elijah was taken up in a whirlwind, so Elisha had to be looking up in order to see him. You see, we will never obtain the anointing by looking earthward with our natural eyes. It is only as we look up and see with supernatural eyes, that the anointing is released.

'Let us fix our eyes on Jesus.'   (Hebrews 12:2)

In Acts 7 when Stephen was being stoned, he could have looked down and seen his natural circumstance, but he didn't. The Bible says that he looked up.

'Stephen, full of the Holy Spirit looked up to heaven, and saw the glory of God, and Jesus standing at the right hand of God.'
(Acts 7:55)

Here we see the result of looking up, no matter what the circumstance may look like. If we will look up, we will see the glory of God. Elisha was being told if you want the anointing, look up, look to the source of the anointing.

Elijah knew that if Elisha was looking heavenwards, then he would be able to handle the responsibility of the new anointing. We will only handle the anointing correctly by constantly looking to Jesus.

When Elisha looked up, he saw that he was about to receive the new anointing and the Bible says:

'... he took hold of his own clothes and tore them apart.'
(2 Kings 2:12)

In other words he tore the old to make room for the new. God will never fill old dirty vessels with new wine. The old has to be torn apart and replaced with the new. To receive the fullness of God, the old man, our old nature, has to be thrown off; everything we've been for so long has to come off, so we can pick up a new mantle.

'Let us throw off everything that hinders.'   (Hebrews 12:1)

Are there things in your life that hinder the fullness of God being able to flow through you? Throw them off! Until we throw off, we can never pick up!

'He picked up the cloak that had fallen from Elijah.'
(2 Kings 2:13)

We see here, that whatever God gives has to be received by us. God did not put the mantle on Elisha, but he put it within his reach. Elisha still had to go and pick up the mantle that he had desired. Many times in the Bible God says 'I have given **but** now you go and get it.'

'See I have given you this land, go in and take possession of the land.' (Deuteronomy 1:8)

God had already given the land, but they never received it, because they were afraid to go in and take hold of it.

Today God has put a new anointing within your reach, but you need to go and pick it up. After Elisha had picked up the mantle, the Bible says that he went back and stood at the Jordan. The Jordan is symbolic of the place of the Spirit. It was where the Israelites crossed over into the Promised Land. I believe that in order to maintain our anointing, we need to constantly be at the place of the Holy Spirit. We need to know him intimately.

'Then he took the cloak that had fallen from him and struck the water with it.' (2 Kings 2:14)

The most important thing of all, is that after you have picked up the anointing, you need to use it. So many Christians say that they have an anointing, and yet they sit at home and do nothing with it. The anointing is given to be used. It is not to make you feel good, it is given so that you can extend the Kingdom of God.

'When he struck the water, it divided to the right and to the left and he crossed over.' (2 Kings 2:14)

When you step out in faith and put the anointing into action, God will make a way where there seems no way. As Elisha used his new anointing, the way opened up for him and he crossed over into new pastures. You may see obstacles in your way right now that stop you from serving God, but if you will step out and use the anointing, then the obstacles will move out of your way and you'll cross over.

Every time in the Bible, when waters parted, it symbolised a new beginning.

'Moses stretched out his hand over the sea, and all that night the Lord drove the sea back with a strong east wind and turned it into dry land.'   (Exodus 14:21)

God parted the waters so that the Israelites could be free from their enemies and the oppression they had been under. When God parted the seas, it was their deliverance, their freedom, their new beginning. They crossed over from oppression to freedom. But notice something interesting here.

'As Pharoah approached, the Israelites looked up and there were the Egyptians marching after them. They were terrified and cried out to the Lord.'   (Exodus 14:10)

Here we see, that even after the Israelites thought they were on their way to safety, out of Egypt, that the Egyptians were still after them. Upon seeing the chariots pursuing them, they became afraid and cried out to the Lord. But look at the Lord's response to Moses.

'Why are you crying out to me? Tell the Israelites to move on. Raise your staff, and stretch out your hand over the sea to divide the water.'   (Exodus 14:15–16)

God was saying, why are you crying out to me? Use what I have given you. The staff was a symbol of the power of God, a symbol of the anointing, and Moses had to use it. It was only as Moses stretched out his hand, that God moved in the situation. If we will pick up the anointing and use it, then we will see God move in our situations. After Moses used the anointing, God destroyed the enemy.

'During the last watch of the night, the Lord looked down from the pillar of fire and cloud at the Egyptian Army, and threw it into confusion. He made the wheels of their chariots come off, so that they had difficulty driving.'   (Exodus 14:24)

One of the things that happens when you use the anointing of God, is that it causes panic and confusion among the enemy.

'Let's get away from the Israelites! The Lord is fighting for them against Egypt.' (Exodus 14:25)

When the enemy realises that he has been stripped of his power by the anointing, he will flee. Under the anointing we can knock the Devil's wheels off!

Do you want to be free from the oppression of the enemy? Do you want the enemy to flee from your life? Do you want God to make a way where there seems no way?

Then pick up the anointing and use it.

'I am making a way in the desert.' (Isaiah 43:19)

God will make a way when we take the authority that we have been given, and use it. Too often we stand crying out in despair to God, when what we should be doing is raising our staff against the enemy. God has given us power over the enemy, we are not poor down-trodden Christians; the Bible says that we are royalty, who are seated in heavenly places with Christ, and everything is under our feet. When Jesus sent out his disciples, he did not say to them 'if you find sick people on your journey, then cry out to me.' No! He said:

'He called his twelve disciples to him and gave them authority to drive out evil spirits and to heal every disease and sickness.'

(Matthew 10:1)

'Heal the sick who are there.' (Luke 10:9)

Jesus gave them the authority over evil spirits, and over every disease and sickness. He expected that if they found sick people anywhere they would use the given power and authority to heal them. Jesus has given to us that same power and authority and we need to use it. If the enemy comes against you or someone you know, then don't cry out 'oh God, what shall I do?' Instead, take authority over that demonic sickness, and command it in the name of Jesus to leave their body. If sickness comes against you as a believer, then rebuke it, and tell it, 'you have no right in or on my body. I am a child of God and by the stripes of Jesus I am healed.' I urge you this day to no longer accept sickness, because Jesus carried all your sicknesses on the cross, and the Devil has no right to put on you what Jesus has already carried and paid for. The Devil can only steal from you what you don't know is yours, and healing is yours, it rightfully belongs to you. If the Devil has stolen it from you, then take it back today!

The Bible says that people are destroyed because of a lack of knowledge. When Jesus was in the wilderness, the way that he overcame the Devil was by quoting the word and it is the same way that we overcome as well. In order for you to be able to use the anointing effectively, you need to know what the Bible says about the promises of God, and the things that rightfully belong to you as a child of God. I encourage you to find out what belongs to you. Ask the Holy Spirit to bring revelation to you concerning the promises of God, so that you can use the anointing to live in the fullness that God has for you, no longer to accept second best, and be robbed and cheated by the Devil.

When you pick up and use the anointing of God, then the waters will part and all obstacles will move. The enemy will panic and become confused and flee from you; his power in your life will be broken, and the power of God in your life will be released.

When Jesus said in Luke 24:19 – *'You shall be clothed with power,'* he was speaking of a new mantle, a new anointing. Elijah had a symbol of the power of God, but we have the real thing. We need to throw off our old self, so that we can be clothed with the Holy Spirit.

Endued

The KJV says *'endued with power.'* To endue means 'to invest'. Do you realise that God has placed an investment in us, and one day he is coming to collect it with interest? In Matthew 25 Jesus told a parable about the talents. The master gave talents to certain men while he went away on a journey, and when he returned he wanted to know what the servants had done with their talents. Some of them had multiplied their talents and they were put in charge of many things. Yet one servant had hidden his talent and when his master returned, he handed the unused talent back. The master became angry, and ordered that the worthless servant be thrown outside.

Jesus has invested in us the Holy Spirit and many different gifts which he expects us to use. One day Jesus will return and ask us 'What did you do with my investment?' Will we be able to say 'Look master, I have gained five more' or will we have to say 'I hid your talent Lord.'?

We can see from the story of Elijah's mantle, seven main steps to receiving a new anointing:

1. Be faithful in another's ministry; Elisha served as Elijah's attendant.
2. Have a hungry heart, and refuse to stay where you are; Elijah told Elisha to stay where he was, but he knew there was more.
3. Look heavenwards, keep your eyes fixed on Jesus.
4. Throw off everything that hinders.
5. Pick up the new anointing.
6. Stand at the Jordan – symbol of the Spirit. A new anointing will only be maintained by knowing the Holy Spirit.
7. Use the new anointing in faith and boldness.

Chapter 4

Your Ministry Partner

As you allow the Holy Spirit to be your senior ministry partner, you will start to see things happening, but we also need to be so sensitive to him.

On several nights at a recent mission, the Holy Spirit changed the whole programme. One night in particular stands out as an example. There was such an awesome sense of the presence of the Holy Spirit, that I began to feel that things might not go to plan. When it came to the part where we would normally take the offering, I looked and saw people so touched by the Lord that I didn't dare step in to take an offering. The Lord honoured this decision as two nights later, the offering was way above what we would normally expect. When we put him first, he always gives back. Anyway, on this night we continued in worship, and I was even debating whether I needed to preach, or if God was just going to move without me doing anything. I decided to speak briefly, just sharing about how Jesus wanted to heal people, and then I felt the Holy Spirit telling me to 'be quiet' and just call the people for healing. It was a very special night with people coming for healing and fresh anointings.

I have also found that the Holy Spirit moves in so many different ways. Sometimes it will be in a very gentle and quiet way, and the presence can be so awesome that you hardly dare speak a word to break the stillness of the Spirit. On other occasions he moves in a much faster and louder way, and if you don't move quickly you can miss what he is doing. We can never predict how or what the Holy Spirit is going to do, which is why we must be so sensitive to him at all times, to make sure we flow with him, not against him. I have also noticed that he will not strive with us; if we yield, he'll move, if we resist he'll withdraw. Even someone in a meeting doing or saying the wrong thing can seem to lessen the presence of the Holy Spirit. Why is this? I don't know. All I know is that I want to be sensitive and allow him to move – don't you?

He Will Tell You Where to Go and What to Say

In Acts 8, we read the story of Philip and the Ethiopian Eunuch. First of all God sends an angel to direct Philip to where he should be going:

> *'Go south to the road, the desert road that goes down from Jerusalem to Gaza.'* (Acts 8:26)

As Philip goes in obedience to the leading of God, he comes across the Ethiopian Eunuch.

> *'The Spirit told Philip, go to the chariot and stay near it.'*
> (Acts 8:29)

Here we see it is now the Holy Spirit who was telling Philip what to do.

> *'Philip ran to the chariot.'* (Acts 8:30)

As well as Philip hearing the natural words of the Holy Spirit, he must have also recognised the sense of urgency in the voice of the Holy Spirit. This is something that cannot be explained in words, but as you get to know the Holy Spirit you will recognise his tone of voice, indicating whether there is an urgency in what he has said. Sometimes there is a time to wait in the Spirit, sometimes a time to walk in the Spirit, and sometimes a time to run in the Spirit. Philip here sensed the urgency and he ran to the chariot.

He sees the Eunuch reading the passage of Isaiah the prophet and asks him:

> *'Do you understand what you are reading?'* (Acts 8:30)

The Eunuch replies:

> *'How can I, unless someone explains it to me?'* (Acts 8:31)

and he invited Philip to come up and sit with him.

We see here that the scriptures are veiled without the help of the Holy Spirit. The Eunuch was unable to understand what he was reading, but Philip under the anointing of the Holy Spirit had the interpretation. Many people in the world today are looking for answers to things that they do not understand, and we who have the interpretation through the Holy Spirit, need to explain them to them. The Holy Spirit led Philip at the right time to a heart that was wanting to know and ready to receive. If we allow the Holy Spirit to guide us, we will find ourselves bearing more fruit because we will be in the right place at the right time. The result of Philip following the Holy Spirit was that the Eunuch was converted and in verse 36 it says *'Look, here is water, why shouldn't I be baptised?'*

I believe that there are three main areas involved in allowing the Holy Spirit to direct us:
1. Go where I tell you;
2. Go when I tell you;
3. Do what I tell you.

Often we make our biggest mistakes because we only listen to one of the instructions, and not all of them. Sometimes we do go where we've been told but not at the right time, or we go at the right time, but don't do the right thing when we get there. The result of this is that we do not see God's plan fulfilled, and we become disillusioned thinking that we misheard God. Although sometimes we might get it wrong, I believe that if we are walking close to God, then we do hear the voice of God most of the time, but sometimes we don't wait for the full instructions. Let's look at these three points:

Go Where I Tell You

Peter had a good idea!

> *'I am going out to fish.'*   (John 21:3)

The others said,

> *'We'll go with you.'*   (John 21:3)

Peter had a good idea and the others followed, but it wasn't God's idea. How often we can follow someone else's good idea, without stopping to think about whether it is God's idea. The result of the good idea was:

> *'That night, they caught nothing.'*   (John 21:3)

'Jesus stood on the shore, but they did not realise that it was Jesus.' (John 21:4)

How often do we go out without instructions, and Jesus is standing there all the time waiting to direct us, but we don't even see him because we have been distracted by:

– '**I** am going,'
– '**My** ministry,'
– '**My** idea.'

'I will go and preach' – your idea or God's? Are we doing it for self or God? Has God told us to go?

Eventually Jesus manages to get their attention and calls out to them.

' "Throw your net on the right side and you will find some." When they did, they were unable to haul the net in because of the large number of fish.' (John 21:6)

– I am going – they caught nothing.
– Jesus directing – they caught a multitude.

Are we throwing our nets on the right side? Are we going where we're meant to be going?

For our ministry, the Lord showed me specifically that we should hold Missions along the coastline of the nation. Now if I decide to disregard what the Lord has said and instead hold Missions in every place except the coast, then I cannot expect to see the fullness of God for the ministry. We must find out exactly where we are meant to be going. When we have found out **where** we are meant to be going, then we need to find out **when** we are meant to be going.

I also believe that if we are in a place of allowing the Holy Spirit to lead us, that he is able to quite easily re-direct us if we are going the wrong way. Sometimes it is good to wait for guidance, but sometimes it can be used as an excuse to do nothing. So many times you hear people say 'It's not God's time to evangelise yet.' Well, I don't believe we have to ask God if we need to evangelise. He told us in his Word to '**go**' and we only need to look at the state of the world to see the desperate need for the Gospel. I believe there are some things that God will never speak audibly about, because they are so obvious, and one of those things is evangelism.

'Paul and his companions travelled throughout the region of Phrygia and Galatia, having been kept by the Holy Spirit from preaching the word in the province of Asia. When they came to the border of Mysia, they tried to enter Bithynia but the Spirit of Jesus would not allow them to.' (Acts 16:6)

Here we see Paul travelling from region to region preaching the Gospel, and one day the Holy Spirit stops him from entering a certain place. Then we see that he has a dream, in which he has a vision of a man of Macedonia saying 'Come over and help us.'

'After Paul had seen the vision, he got ready at once to leave for Macedonia, concluding that God had called us to preach the Gospel to them.' (Acts 16:10)

We see that because of the close fellowship that Paul must have had with the Holy Spirit, and because of his obedience, he was able to re-direct Paul to the place where he wanted him to be.

Therefore I believe that although we seek guidance, we also don't need to constantly worry about whether we are in the right place. If we truly want to be in the right place and we are seeking and serving God, then God will even along the way make things perfectly clear to us, and he is able to re-direct us if we are not in the place that he wants us to be.

Go When I Tell You

We often think 'Oh God said "Go to America," so I will go tomorrow' and we dash off so fast that God doesn't have a chance to speak any more instructions. So, we dash off to America and when we get there, it doesn't work the way we thought it would, so we come home totally discouraged, concluding that we never heard the voice of God. The more likely truth though, is that you did hear the voice of God, but you only received half the instructions. We live in an instant world and we want to hear God 'now, now, now' but often we have to take time and listen patiently to get all the details from God.

- If we go too soon – we miss it.
- If we go too late – we miss it.
- If we go on time – we find it.

When Jesus was preparing for the Last Supper, he sent his disciples to make the preparations:

'Go into the city and a man carrying a water jar will meet you. Follow him.' (Mark 14:13)

They were to follow the man with the water jar to the house where the Supper was to be held. Now, what would have happened if the disciples had thought 'Well, shall we go this afternoon or maybe later on?' They had to go at the exact time Jesus told them in order to meet the man with the water jar. This man with the water jar was not hanging around all day, waiting for disciples to turn up.

Half of us would probably have gone 'whenever we felt like it' and then come back and said, 'But Lord, there was no man carrying a water jar!' I wonder how many times we've missed the water jar because we went at the wrong time.

God has always had a sense of 'The Right Time'. In Leviticus 16 we read:

'The Lord said to Moses; tell your brother Aaron not to come whenever he chooses into the most holy place behind the curtain, in front of the atonement cover on the ark, or else he will die.' (Leviticus 16:2)

Aaron was given specific instructions as to when and how he was to enter the most holy place, and if he didn't do as he was told, he would die. To step out of the will of God is to place ourselves in a dangerous place.

The Israelites were told to take possession of the Promised Land, but they went at the wrong time and they missed it.

'See the Lord your God has given you the land. Go up and take possession of it as the Lord, the God of your fathers told you. Do not be afraid, do not be discouraged.' (Deuteronomy 1:21)

God was saying that he had already given them the land, but they needed to go and take it. God assured them of his constant protection and of the victory that was already theirs, but despite all of this, they chose to look with their natural eyes instead of listening to what God had said. Instead of remembering the promises of God, they saw the giants in the land instead.

'The people are stronger and taller than we are.'
                                        (Deuteronomy 1:28)

They had forgotten the promises of God and allowed fear to come in. How often we too can easily forget what God has said as soon as a problem arises.

'You were unwilling to go up, you rebelled against the command of the Lord your God.'   (Deuteronomy 1:26)

Because of the disobedience of the people, the ones responsible for spreading the bad report were struck down and killed, and the rest of the Israelites wandered in the wilderness for forty years, instead of crossing into the Promised Land. I wonder how often we wander in circles instead of enjoying the promises of God, because of our disobedience. When the people realised the mistake that they had made they said:

'"We have sinned ... we will go up to the place the Lord promised." But Moses said, "Why are you disobeying the Lord's command? This will not succeed! Do not go up, because the Lord is not with you."'   (Numbers 14:40–41)

They had missed their chance! Now that they had realised their mistake, they thought that they could still go but they'd missed the timing of God. God told them not to go, it was too late, they had missed it. But still in their presumption the Bible says they went anyway and they were defeated by their enemies. They thought that it did not matter what time they went, but it did. God had set a specific time for them to go, but they disobeyed, and when they did decide to go, the Bible says:

'Neither Moses nor the ark of the Lord's covenant moved from the camp.'   (Numbers 14:44)

The Ark was a symbol of the presence of God. They moved out against the enemy without the presence of God, and disaster struck. In Exodus 23:15 the prayer of Moses was:

'If your presence does not go with us, do not send us up from here.'

When Moses saw that the presence was not going, he didn't move. If we march off in presumption without the presence of God, then we are in danger. We need to live like Ezekiel 1:12:

'Wherever the Spirit would go, they would go without turning as they went.'

As you allow the Holy Spirit to be your ministry partner, he will lead and guide you and wherever he goes, you'll go, without looking to the right or to the left as you go.

Do What I Tell You

After we have found out where we are meant to be going and when we are meant to be going, we then need to know what we are meant to be doing when we get there.

'See I have delivered Jericho into your hands.'   (Joshua 6:2)

Again, we see God saying these famous words 'see I have given you.' God was telling Joshua that he had given the city into his hands, but then he was also given the instructions on how he was to take the city. Sometimes the way God may tell you to do something isn't what you would have chosen or thought.

'March around the city, once with all the armed men. Do this for six days ... On the seventh day, march around the city seven times, with the priests blowing the trumpets.'

(Joshua 6:3–4)

Imagine how strange this must have looked; a whole week and all they did was march around blowing trumpets, but Joshua led the people in obedience to the Lord's command. Joshua was there when the Israelites missed the Promised Land through their disobedience, and so he had probably decided never to miss the promises of God again. Joshua was a man who knew the presence of God and was seen as a great leader and warrior.

'The seventh time around when the priests sounded the trumpet blast, Joshua commanded the people, "Shout! For the Lord has given you the city!'   (Joshua 6:16)

'When the trumpets sounded, the people shouted, and at the sound of the trumpet, when the people gave a loud shout, the wall collapsed; so every man charged straight in, and they took the city.'   (Joshua 6:20)

Because of Joshua's obedience to the Lord's specific instructions, the people were able to take the city and win the victory. Sometimes God may tell us to do things which seem strange, but we need to act in obedience to what he has said. In the same way as obedience brings victory, so also disobedience brings defeat.

> *'Keep away from the devoted things, so that you will not bring about your own destruction.'*   (Joshua 6:18)

There were very specific instructions given that after they had taken the city, they were not allowed to touch the devoted things.

> *'But the Israelites acted unfaithfully in regard to the devoted things; Achan son of Carmi ... took some of them. So the Lord's anger burned against Israel.'*   (Joshua 7:1)

Achan had taken some of the devoted things and hidden them for himself. Because of this, the wrath of God came upon the whole of the camp. When the Israelites went up to fight against Ai, we see that they were defeated. They had just won an enormous battle at Jericho and now at Ai, which would seem easy in comparison, they are defeated. Joshua falls down on his face, crying out before the Lord and asking why he has allowed this defeat after such a great victory. The answer comes back:

> *'Israel has sinned ... They have taken some of the devoted things; they have stolen, they have lied, they have put them with their own possessions. That is why the Israelites cannot stand against their enemies.'*   (Joshua 7:11–12)

We see that because of their disobedience to what the Lord had told them, they were unable to stand against the enemy. When we do what God tells us to do, it will mean victory but when we don't, it will mean defeat. It was not until after they had destroyed Achan, that they were able to go and gain victory at Ai.

So, we need to be led by the Holy Spirit as to where we are going, when we are going and what we are doing or saying when we get there.

How Can We Know What To Do or Say in a Situation?

'Whenever you are arrested and brought to trial, do not worry beforehand about what to say. Just say whatever is given you at the time, for it is not you speaking, but the Holy Spirit.'

(Mark 13:11)

Although the scripture here is referring to being arrested, I also believe that the Holy Spirit will give us the words to say in any situation where they are needed.

'Ah Sovereign Lord, I do not know how to speak, I am only a child.'   (Jeremiah 1:6)

God had spoken to Jeremiah, telling him that he was appointed as a prophet to the nations. Understandably this shocked Jeremiah, who it seems felt inadequate for the job. It is interesting how all the way through the Bible, God chooses people who felt inadequate. Maybe this is so his power could be shown more.

'Then the Lord reached out his hand and touched my mouth, and said to me "Now I have put my words in your mouth."'

(Jeremiah 1:9)

Whenever we speak for God, we don't need to worry about what to say, for if we ask him, then he will put his words in our mouths.

'Open wide your mouth and I will fill it.'   (Psalm 81:10)

In order for God's words to be able to flow from our mouths, we need to open them in faith. Many times I have stood to preach not knowing what I was about to say. At a recent meeting, I had gone with a gospel message prepared, but suddenly the Holy Spirit said 'Change it, talk about the anointing.' Inside I began having a hasty conversation with the Holy Spirit. 'Lord, what scripture? What do you want me to share?' Then I said 'OK, I will open my mouth but you need to give me something to say.' Needless to say he did give me something to say, but you see, the step of faith is opening your mouth. The words will never be given while we keep quiet, we have to take the first step, and then the rest will flow. Often when the interpretation of a tongue is given to someone, the

Holy Spirit will only give one line of the interpretation, and it is only as you begin to speak that one line, that the rest flows out as well. Maybe a lot of people keep quiet because they don't feel they have enough of the interpretation, not realising that they need to give what they have in faith, and then God will give them the rest.

No matter what situation we may face, we need to be totally dependent on the Holy Spirit to tell us what to say or do in a situation. Not only does he give us the words to say, but he has made all the gifts of the Spirit available to us.

The gifts of the Spirit as listed in 1 Corinthians 12 are:

Wisdom, message of knowledge, faith, healings, miracles, prophecy, discernment of spirits, tongues, interpretation of tongues.

I believe that although some people may seem to move in a particular gift more frequently than others, all the gifts are available to any believer at certain times, and for certain situations. I believe that every believer needs to ask for the gift of wisdom.

'If any of you lacks wisdom, he should ask God who gives generously to all.'   (James 1:5)

In situations that we face every day, we need to have the wisdom of God.

When the Lord appeared to Solomon, he said,

'Ask for whatever you want me to give you.'   (2 Chronicles 1:7)

I wonder what our response would have been if God had said to us 'Ask whatever you want.' I wonder what we would have asked for. Would you have asked for wisdom?

'Give me wisdom and knowledge, that I may lead this people.'
(2 Chronicles 1:10)

'God said to Solomon, "Since this is your heart's desire and you haven't asked for wealth, riches or honour, nor for the death of your enemies, and since you have not asked for a long life but for wisdom and knowledge to govern my people over whom I have made you king, therefore wisdom and knowledge will be given you. And I will also give you wealth, riches and honour, such

*as no king who was before you ever had and none after you will
have.'* (2 Chronicles 1:11–12)

Solomon had a right heart attitude and asked for wisdom
instead of riches, so he received both.

*'Seek first his kingdom and righteousness and all these things will
be given to you as well.'* (Matthew 6:33)

If we want to know what we are meant to be doing, then we
need to ask God for wisdom. Many will come and try to deceive
you, to take you along the wrong pathway, but you need to
know the voice of God and the wisdom of God. At this point
let me add in here about taking and listening to advice from
other people, concerning the way that you should go.

*'Listen to advice and accept instruction and in the end you will be
wise.'* (Proverbs 19:20)

'Make plans by seeking advice, if you wage war, obtain guidance.'
(Proverbs 20:18)

The Bible clearly states that it is good to listen to advice, and
that the gifts of the word of knowledge and prophecy were
given for this purpose. However, I would like to share a few
points here. Make sure that the person who you accept the
advice from, is a godly person who you know spends time in
the presence of God. Too often, we can end up confused
because we listen to advice that is of the flesh and not of
God. In the same way as God sends people to advise us, so the
Devil sends people to confuse us. Secondly, always check
everything out with the Holy Spirit, even if it is the most godly
person in the church who has said it. We can sometimes be
naive as Christians and as soon as a godly person says something we say 'Oh the Lord hath spoken,' and sometimes 'the
Lord hath spoken nothing.' I am not saying that we become
arrogant and do not listen, but the Bible says;

'Test everything.' (1 Thessalonians 5:21)

Whenever a person who I respect in the Lord says something,
my response is 'OK, Lord, this is what Fred said, now Lord,
what do you have to say about this?'

We need to make sure that we are hearing from God, and not
people's opinions. It amazes me how there can be some people

who never spend time with God, and then come to a godly person and say 'the Lord hath said, you are not in the will of God!' God sums this up in Jeremiah 23:32:

> *'They lead my people astray with their reckless lies, yet I did not send them or appoint them.'*

> *'I am against the prophets who wag their own tongues and yet declare "The Lord declares."'*   (Jeremiah 23:31)

So we see that we need the wisdom and discernment of God to be able to know the truth of what God is saying. It is good to listen to advice, and in fact the Bible says it is wisdom to do so, but we also need to be careful who we listen to, and to test everything directly with the Holy Spirit. If you are in confusion right now over a situation, then confusion is not from God, it is from the Devil. When we are confused, we are spiritually paralysed. The enemy does not want us to be clear-minded about where we are going, so he sends confusion. If this is you now, then I want you to bind the spirit of confusion over your life right now in the name of Jesus, and ask God to loose clarity and truth into your mind. If you are confused because you have asked many people for advice, then I want you to put aside all their opinions and to seek the voice of the Holy Spirit until you get his answer. God promises this in his word.

> *'I am the Lord your God who teaches you what is best for you, who directs you in the way you should go.'*   (Isaiah 48:17)

Although God may use people to guide and advise you, ultimately it is God who will guide you in the way that you should go. Our aim should be that we become so close to God, and so sensitive to the voice of the Holy Spirit, that we will automatically know which is the right way.

How Can We Know the Will of God?

You may desire to earnestly serve God and to be in the centre of his will, and now you ask; how can I know the will of God for my life?

> *'For I know the plans I have for you, declares the Lord.'*
>   (Jeremiah 29:11)

This scripture was the very first passage that the Lord gave to me when I became a Christian. Isn't it wonderful to know that the Lord has a plan for our lives and he planned it all before the creation of the world. You were not a mistake! God created you and chose you for a purpose. God has a plan and a purpose for our lives, but I believe it is up to us whether that plan is fulfilled or not. We have the choice whether to walk in the will of God or not, and unfortunately so many people chose not to, and miss the plan that God has for their lives.

Ephesians is what I call 'The Destiny Book.'

'For he chose us in him before the creation of the world.'

(Ephesians 1:4)

Not only before you were born, but even before the creation of the world God knew all about you, and he chose you to be set apart for him.

'For we are God's workmanship, created in Christ Jesus to do good works, which God prepared in advance for us to do.'

(Ephesians 2:10)

Not only were we chosen before the creation of the world, but the calling upon our lives was also decided before the creation of the world. Do you realise what the passage means when it says, *'We are God's workmanship'*? Let me explain, so that you can understand exactly what is being said here, and I believe it will transform your life. If, for example, I am a carpenter and I make a wardrobe, then that wardrobe is my workmanship, it is what I have created and I have created it with a purpose in mind – the purpose being to hang clothes in it. Now the wardrobe was made specifically to hang clothes in, and is only of any use if that is what it is used for. It wouldn't be of any use as a dining room table, because that was not what it was designed for.

If I was a potter and I created a vase, I would make it a certain shape and with the ability to be able to hold water, so I could put my flowers in it.

Now in the same way when God created you, he had a specific purpose for you in mind and he created you with the exact personality, character, strengths, abilities, to be able to be used for the purpose he had in mind. Doesn't that give you a sense of worth and purpose? So often, the Devil destroys Christians by telling them, 'You're no good, you're too shy, too weak, you don't have this or that.' Today, you can tell the Devil that he is a liar, because when God created you, he made you perfect for the task he had in mind. Now, all you have to do is find out what the will and purpose of God is for your life.

> *'No-one knows the thoughts of God except the Spirit of God.'*
> (1 Corinthians 2:11)

The Holy Spirit knows the thoughts of God; he knows the will of God. The Holy Spirit not only knows the will of God, but he desires to share it with you, if you will open your ears to his voice.

> *'But when he the Spirit of truth comes, he will guide you into all truth.'*   (John 16:13)

The Devil brings confusion and lies, but the Holy Spirit brings truth. He is truth and if you will listen and follow him, then he will guide you into all truth; he will guide you into the will of God. Many times in Revelation, we read these words:

> *'He who has an ear, let him hear what the Spirit says to the churches.'*   (Revelation 2:7)

To each of the seven churches that are spoken to, the same words are spoken: *'He who has an ear, let him hear what the Spirit says to the churches.'*

I believe that the Holy Spirit is more willing to speak to us than most of us imagine. I believe that if we had ears to hear, then we would discover that he is speaking all the time.

> *'Be transformed by the renewing of your mind, then you will be able to test and approve what God's will is.'*   (Romans 12:2)

We see here, that a lot of knowing the will of God starts with our minds. It is in our minds that the enemy attacks us most. He sends a whole load of junk and confusion to try to distract us from hearing the voice of the Holy Spirit. You see, while our minds are on other things, we will not be able to hear that gentle whisper of the Holy Spirit, for his voice will be drowned by the loud voices. Very rarely will the Holy Spirit shout to make himself heard. He is a gentleman and if we do not want to listen, he will withdraw. The nagging voice is not God, the voice that pressurises is not God, the voice that brings fear is not God (there is a difference between an awesome fear of God and the fear that the Devil sends). When Elijah was afraid, God told him to go and stand on the mountain, for the Lord was going to pass by.

> *'A great and powerful wind tore the mountains apart and shattered the rocks before the Lord , but the Lord was not in the wind. After the wind there was an earthquake, but the Lord was not in the earthquake. After the earthquake came a fire, but the Lord was not in the fire. And after the fire came a gentle whisper. When Elijah heard it, he pulled his cloak over his face and went out and stood at the mouth of the cave. Then a voice came to him "What are you doing here Elijah?"'* (1 Kings 19:11–13)

The voice of the Holy Spirit is the small still voice, not the big booming voice. You may say, 'how will I know if it is the Holy Spirit speaking?' Well, let me ask you a question – if your best friend phoned you up, would you recognise them, or would you say 'Who is this?' You see, if you know someone, you don't have to ask, 'is that you?' You will know if it is them or not. The enemy will try to deceive you and counterfeit the voice of the Holy Spirit, but if you have a personal and deep relationship with the Holy Spirit, you will not be fooled easily.

> *'Whether you turn to the right or to the left, your ears will hear a voice behind you saying "This is the way, walk in it."'*
> (Isaiah 30:21)

I believe that if you desire to be in the will of God, then you will be, because God will guide and direct you in the way you should go. Listen to the voice of the Holy Spirit and he will tell you the will of God for your life. He may show you in many different ways; it may be just a sense of knowing in your spirit, or it may be a specific word or picture or dream. When God spoke to me about the ministry, I was lying in bed one night and God said to me 'I've called you to preach.' Then after that I began to get a series of pictures where I saw myself standing on a platform preaching. In my experience, I have found that God often shows us an ultimate vision of what he has planned for us, and then he also gives us the plan of how to fulfil the ultimate vision. You see, God has shown to me a vision which is yet to be fulfilled, but I know it will happen one day, as long as I stay in the will of God. It is this vision that keeps me going when things are tough. Instead of staying discouraged, I have the strength to press on, because God has shown me there is something greater ahead. No matter what people may say, or no matter what the circumstances look like, I can say 'God said it will happen, and I'm pressing on.' That's why God gives us dreams and visions; so that we have a hope to hold on to, a purpose to move forward, something to aim for. But there also need to be constant visions which take us towards the ultimate vision; we need to know what we are meant to be doing now, at this present time, and this again is by a constant daily relationship with the Holy Spirit.

Joseph was a young man who had a dream, and yet we see that it was a long time before the dream was fulfilled, and he had to go through many trials on the way. By the time he was falsely accused and thrown into prison, he could have quite easily forgotten the dream, but he didn't and the dream was fulfilled. When God gives you a dream or vision, you need to hold onto it despite all the opposition that may come against you. People may be jealous of you because they don't have a dream as well.

> *'Joseph had a dream and when he told it to his brothers, they hated him all the more.'*   (Genesis 37:5)

Having a dream will not always make you popular and you need to be discerning as to who you share the dream with.

> *'His brothers were jealous of him.'*   (Genesis 37:11)

Two things can happen when you get a dream from God:
1. Other Christians can become jealous and try to bring discouragement to you.
2. The Devil will try to kill the dream, and often it can be by using other Christians to criticise.

In situations like this, you need to know whom you have believed, and stand firm in what God has told you. Sometimes it is good to be like Mary.

> *'Mary treasured up all these things and pondered them in her heart.'*   (Luke 2:19)

After the birth of Jesus, the shepherds spread the news all over the place about what the angels had said about the child, but Mary however just pondered the things in her heart.

Although it is good to share with others what God has said, it is also good sometimes to just ponder things in our heart.

'Here comes that dreamer. Come now let's kill him, then we'll see what comes of his dreams.' (Genesis 37:19)

They wanted to kill the dream because they were jealous. Joseph however was not killed, but was sold into Egypt, but despite all of this, the dream was fulfilled twenty years later. You can read the story of Joseph from Genesis 37 right through to the fulfilment of the dream in Genesis 42. The parable of the story is to hold onto your dream, hold on to what God has said, no matter what the circumstances may look like around you. The only person who can stop the will of God for your life is you, by refusing to walk in the will of God. But if you desire the will of God, then no man or demon can stop it.

Chapter 5

What Difference Will Knowing the Holy Spirit Make?

You Will Stop Striving

Are you the type of person who strives to make things happen and then gets frustrated because they don't? Maybe you've been trying to do things in your own strength and ability instead of allowing the Holy Spirit to take control.

'Not by might, nor by power but by my Spirit says the Lord.'
(Zechariah 4:6)

We cannot achieve things by our own efforts but only by the Holy Spirit. If we could make things happen by our own efforts, then we would not need God, and our dependence on God would vanish. The moment we depend on self, all anointing goes out the window.

Often when God calls us to do something, it is something which in our natural abilities we cannot do. Why? Because if we could do it in our natural ability, we wouldn't need to rely on God. But when we rely on God, he turns our natural ability into a supernatural one. In my natural ability I am not a preacher. If I tried to speak without the help of the Holy Spirit I would not be able to think of two words to say, because my natural personality is to be quiet and certainly not to be able to get up in front of lots of people. **But** the anointing of the Holy Spirit gives you boldness and the words to say. Under the anointing you become a different person and do things you never thought were possible.

Anything that we try to do by striving will fail, because it is an act of the flesh and not of the Spirit. That doesn't mean that we become lazy and do nothing, but what it means is that we do our best with the help of the Holy Spirit, doing his will and not our own.

He'll Change Your Prayer Life

Have you ever started to pray and then not been able to think what to pray about? Or maybe there are so many things to pray about that you don't know how or where to start. The Bible says in Romans 8:26–27:

'The Spirit helps us in our weakness. We do not know what we ought to pray for, but the Spirit himself intercedes for us with groans that words cannot express. And he who searches our hearts knows the mind of the Spirit, because the Spirit intercedes for the saints in accordance with God's will.'

Here the Bible quite clearly states that without the Holy Spirit we will struggle to pray – we don't know how to pray. The disciples once said to Jesus *'Lord teach us to pray.'* I believe that Jesus has given us the greatest teacher to help us to pray. In 1 John 5:14 we read:

'If we ask anything according to his will he hears us and if we know that he hears us, whatever we ask – we know that we have what we asked of him.'

We can ask for anything that is in the will of God and we will receive it. The main problem here, is that so often we struggle to know what the will of God is, so how can we pray in the will of God if we don't know what that is? Often our prayers are more luck than judgement, so to speak, more praying in hope instead of praying in faith. If we knew the will of God, I believe we would pray more earnestly and with more boldness than we have done before. So how can we know the will of God? The answer lies in Romans 8:27 – the Holy Spirit knows the will of God!

'No-one knows the thoughts of God, except the Spirit of God.'
(1 Corinthians 2:11)

The Holy Spirit knows the thoughts of God. If you were convinced that someone living in your street knew the will of God for your life, would you not want to go and speak to them? The Holy Spirit knows the will of God for your life and every situation, and as you speak to him, he will reveal that to you too.

Imagine coming to a place in God where you were finding all your prayers being answered, instead of wondering if you were talking into thin air. When we pray in the will of God, we will get positive answers.

I challenge you next time you go to pray to say, 'Holy Spirit, I welcome you, I don't know what to pray for, will you please help me.' I believe that your prayer life will be transformed, no longer will you struggle to pray for ten minutes, twenty minutes, half an hour. Maybe you've thought it was an impossibility to pray for an hour, but I tell you, once you get to know the Holy Spirit and welcome him into your prayer times, an hour will only just cover the 'having a chat' time, and you will still need more time to really pray. When you get to know the Holy Spirit, the relationship will become so personal that you will be able to talk to God about anything and everything. Sometimes there are things that you can share with no-one, especially when you are in ministry, but you can share them with the Holy Spirit. You will come to a place where you will want to extend your prayer time just so that you can have heart-to-heart talks with the Holy Spirit. I have discovered that I can be so real with him. If I'm feeling low about something, I don't have to make out that everything is fine when I come to pray. Often I find myself sharing the problem with the Holy Spirit, and we have a chat and he speaks to me and comforts me and then after that we talk about what we should pray for. So often many people go with their problems to many counsellors, and yet how often do we go to 'the Counsellor' – the Holy Spirit. Human counsellors can give many opinions but 'the Counsellor' will only give the truth.

The Bible states in John 16:13:

> *'But when he the Spirit of truth comes, he will guide you into all truth; he will not speak on his own, he will speak only what he hears and he will tell you what is yet to come.'*

The Holy Spirit is the one who will speak into our lives the will of the Father. He does not speak his own will differently to the Father and Jesus. The Bible says that *'he will speak only what he hears.'*

Do you ever find that you run out of words, not knowing how to pray into a situation? Many times I have gone to pray for a particular person or situation, and found that I am very limited in my normal language to know what to pray. After praying 'Lord bless them, help them Lord,' etc., we can sometimes become stuck to know what else to specifically pray. It is here again that the Holy Spirit will help us. Often I will say 'Holy Spirit, you know the will of God for this situation, help me now to pray for this person or situation.' It is then that I am able to pray in the heavenly language that the Lord has given. If you are reading this and you have never experienced praying in a heavenly language sometimes referred to as 'tongues,' then right now, ask God to release that gift to you.

The Bible says in Luke 11:13:

'How much more will your Father in heaven give the Holy Spirit to those who ask him.'

John the Baptist referred to Jesus as one who would *'Baptise with the Holy Spirit and with fire'* (Matthew 3:11). One of the gifts listed in 1 Corinthians 12 is speaking in different kinds of tongues. This gift is given by the Holy Spirit for our edification, and to enable us to pray directly to God.

Our Teacher

Not only will the Holy Spirit change your prayer life, but he will also make the Word of God come alive to you. Have you ever read a passage of scripture that is very familiar to you, but then one day you read it and it seems to jump out at you, and you suddenly see a revelation that you never noticed before? Why has that piece of scripture suddenly come alive and taken on a totally new meaning? the Bible says that *'he will teach you all things'* (John 14:26). Without the help of the Holy Spirit the scriptures are veiled, and we cannot receive the truth that God wants us to see. After Jesus had risen from the dead, he appeared to his disciples and walked with them, although at first they did not realise that it was Jesus. Then the Bible says that *'he opened their minds so they could understand the scriptures'* (Luke 24:45). So we see that in the natural we cannot understand the scriptures, we need our minds to be opened. Jesus has left the Holy Spirit here to be our teacher and to give us new and exciting revelations from the very throne of God.

He Will Help You Witness for Jesus

'When he comes, he will convict the world of guilt.' (John 16:8)

When you know the Holy Spirit in your life, it will be easier to witness for Jesus because it is the Holy Spirit who convicts people of their sin, and their need of Jesus. We can speak words to people all day long, but unless the Holy Spirit touches their hearts, they just remain empty words. When you know the Holy Spirit, then your words will carry power, and people's hearts will be touched, and lives will be changed.

When you know and move with the Holy Spirit, he will give you words to speak directly into people's lives and situations.

In 1 Corinthians 12:7–11, we read of some of the gifts of the Spirit which are wisdom, knowledge, faith, healings, miracles, prophecy, discernment of spirits, tongues and interpretation of tongues, and the Bible declares that:

'All these are the work of one and the same Spirit, and he gives them to each one, just as he determines.' (1 Corinthians 12:11)

It is the Holy Spirit who has all of these gifts, and it is his choice who he decides to give them to. Imagine for a minute that you had lots of precious gifts in your keeping, and you could decide who you were going to give them to. Who would you choose? Would you choose people who were close to you? People that you spent a lot of time with? People who you felt would benefit from, and appreciate your gifts? Would you give your gifts to someone who would be ungrateful and abuse your gifts? Most of us would want to give nice gifts to those close to us, and to those who would appreciate and use the gifts given. I believe that in the same way, the Holy Spirit gives his gifts to those who are close to him, and those that he knows will appreciate, and use correctly the gifts that he gives them.

How Do We Receive?

'Eagerly desire the greater gifts.'   (1 Corinthians 12:31)

The gifts will not come to us by accident! Everything that comes from God has to be eagerly desired – *'seek me and you will find me.'* We need to desire all the fullness that God has for us, and we need to ask God for the gifts of the Spirit, that we can use them for his glory.

> *'Ask and it will be given to you.'*   (Luke 11:9)

> *'You do not have because you do not ask God.'*   (James 4:2)

I believe that there are many unclaimed gifts in heaven, because we do not realise that they are there for us, and God is just waiting for us to ask for them.

He Gives Us Spiritual Life

> *'The same Spirit who raised Jesus from the dead shall also quicken our mortal bodies.'*   (Romans 8:11)

In other words, if we do things under the power of the Holy Spirit we should be more energetic when we've finished, than before we started. At a long mission recently, in the natural we were starting to get tired, but then something supernatural started to happen. We were finding that before each meeting we were tired, but by the end of the meeting we had been revitalised, and we stayed up late talking over all the wonderful things that had happened in the meeting! When we minister in the Holy Spirit, he recharges our spiritual batteries with his supernatural power.

In Ezekiel 37 we read the story of the valley of the dry bones. The Bible says, *'There was no breath in them.'* They were dead because there was no breath in them. Do you feel dry? Do you sometimes feel as though there is no spiritual breath in you?

> *'I will make breath enter you and you will come to life.'*
> (Ezekiel 37:5)

The Hebrew word here, can also mean 'wind' or 'spirit'. God was saying, I will breathe the Holy Spirit on you and you will come to life.

> *'I looked and tendons and flesh appeared on them and skin covered them but there was no breath in them.'*   (Ezekiel 37:8)

The first thing that happened as Ezekiel prophesied, was that the physical shape of the man came back together again, but there was still no breath there. In other words, it all looked good on the outside but there was still no life inside. They looked alive, but really they were dead. You know, sometimes that can be a bit like a lot of Christians – everything can look good on the outside, but inside they're spiritually dead; there's no breath there. We can put on our best clothes and make ourselves look nice, but often it can be a disguise for how we are really feeling underneath. Under the beauty there can be pain and heartache, a sense of despair, and although we don't really want anyone to know, at the same time, we are really crying out for someone to notice that we need help.

However it is not always this kind of deadness, sometimes it can be a religious dryness. In other words, we feel as though we've got it all together, we have a nice home and family, and we go to church every week, but it's just a ritual. You go through the same service, sing the same songs, say the same prayers, but there's no real joy and excitement about it. It all looks good to the person looking from the outside, but you and God know that there's no breath in you. You need the Holy Spirit to breathe life into you.

> *'Breath entered them and they stood up on their feet – a vast army.'*   (Ezekiel 37:10)

Hallelujah! When the breath of the Holy Spirit touches you, not only do you come alive but you become someone powerful in the Kingdom of God. One minute they were dead and dry, and the next minute they were a powerful army. Do you want to be a mighty warrior for God? Then let the Holy Spirit breathe on you.

What difference will the Holy Spirit make? He'll make you a mighty warrior instead of being dead and dry.

He'll Give You Boldness

> *'The disciples were together with the doors locked for fear of the Jews.'*   (John 20:19)

After Jesus had been crucified, the disciples were afraid for their own lives, and they locked themselves away. But turn your Bible now about two or three pages and you will see a totally different picture all together.

'Those who accepted his message were baptised and about 3,000 were added to their number that day.' (Acts 2:41)

Just two pages later, Peter, one of the disciples who had previously been scared for his life on more than one occasion, is now preaching a message so boldly that 3,000 people get saved.

What made the difference? What turned the fear into boldness? the answer lies in Acts 2:4: *'All of them were filled with the Holy Spirit.'*

It was the Holy Spirit who changed their fear to boldness.

'They were all filled with the Holy Spirit and spoke the Word of God boldly.' (Acts 4:31)

The Holy Spirit will give you a boldness; a boldness to preach the gospel, a boldness to come against the enemy.

'Suddenly a young lion came roaring towards him. The Spirit of the Lord came upon him in power so that he tore the lion apart with his bare hands.' (Judges 14:5–6)

'Your enemy the Devil prowls around like a roaring lion.'

(James 5:8)

We see that the Devil is referred to as a roaring lion, but with the power of the Holy Spirit upon our lives, we can tear him apart. The Holy Spirit will give us power over the Devil. We will become bold in spiritual warfare when the Holy Spirit is with us.

A Supernatural Strength

'And if the Spirit of him who raised Jesus from the dead is living in you.' (Romans 8:11)

The same power that raised Jesus from the dead is living daily, constantly within you if you know Jesus. Just think for a minute of the significance of what that really means, and the potential it brings. We have the ability and potential to be able to live and move in the supernatural, because the supernatural power of God is living inside us every day. With the super-natural power of God within us, also comes the potential to be an overcomer. Jesus overcame the Devil and the world and all its temptations, and we have been given the same potential, the same Spirit living within us.

'In all these things we are more than conquerors.'

(Romans 8:27)

'How much more will those who receive God's abundant provision of grace and the gift of righteousness reign in life.'

(Romans 5:17)

God has given to us not the potential to survive, but the potential to overcome, and to reign triumphantly in this life. We are not supposed to say 'oh dear, I wonder if I can just survive this situation.' No! You were made to overcome, and to reign above your circumstances. We should never be 'under the circumstances.' In Christ, we are over the circumstances. The indwelling of the Holy Spirit gives us the strength to be an overcomer, not a survivor. To be a warrior not a worrier.

'Heat is reduced by the presence of a cloud.'   (Isaiah 25:5)

In the Old Testament the cloud that the Israelites followed was symbolic of the Holy Spirit. Sometimes we can find ourselves in a situation that is too hot to handle, and all we seem to do is worry about the situation. Here in Isaiah we see the Holy Spirit as the Comforter, the one who takes us out of the heat, and into the refreshing shade.

'With the Holy Spirit, everything is cool!'

You'll Know You're Saved

So many people worry about whether they are truly saved or not. You see the Holy Spirit brings conviction, but the Devil brings condemnation. He whispers in people's ears 'look what you did last week. How can you be saved?' He tries to tell us that when we sin, we have lost our salvation. It is the Holy Spirit who will witness to our Spirit the forgiveness that we require, and the assurance of our salvation.

'The Spirit himself testifies with our spirit that we are children of God.'   (Romans 8:16)

The Holy Spirit will convince us that even if we have made mistakes, as long as we truly love Jesus, then we are a child of God. The Bible says that the Holy Spirit is our deposit, guaranteeing what is to come. In a way the Holy Spirit is our engagement ring.

> *'No eye has seen, no ear has heard, no mind has conceived what God has prepared for those who love him, but God has revealed it to us by his Spirit.'*　　(1 Corinthians 2:9)

The Holy Spirit lets us into the secrets of God. The Holy Spirit, as you fellowship with him, will begin to draw back the curtains and allow you to have a peep at the things that God has in store for you, not only in this life, but in the life to come as well.

> *'The Spirit searches all things, even the deep things of God.'*
>　　　　　　　　　　　　　　　　　　(1 Corinthians 2:10)

The Holy Spirit knows the deep secrets of the heart of God, and as he begins to trust you, he will share some with you.

You'll be Changed Forever

One of the jobs of the Holy Spirit, is to daily make us more like Jesus, until one day we shall be like him. He is working in us, daily changing us; a process known as sanctification.

> *'We who with unveiled faces all reflect the Lord's glory are being transformed into his likeness with every increasing glory which comes from the Lord who is the Spirit.'*　　(2 Corinthians 3:18)

Have you ever looked back over your life and realised that you don't think the same as you used to, that your attitudes are different, the way that you act is different? The things that you used to like doing, you no longer enjoy? Why do you think this is? Is it because you have just become older, and your opinions have changed, or could it be a work of the Holy Spirit within your life? Many people when considering becoming a Christian, ask such questions as 'Will I have to give up certain things to be a Christian?' I have found, that although sometimes there has to be an act of our will to want to change, the main part of the change is done by the Holy Spirit. You find that suddenly the things that you used to enjoy, no longer hold any real meaning. The places that you used to like going to, you now feel out of place in.

'The Spirit of the Lord will come upon you in power, and you will prophesy with them and you will be changed into a different person.' (1 Samuel 10:6)

What difference will the Holy Spirit make? He will change you into a different person. Once you have an encounter with the Holy Spirit, it is impossible to ever be the same person again.

'Where the Spirit of the Lord is there is freedom.'

(2 Corinthians 3:17)

When the Holy Spirit showed up, it symbolised the end of the law, and the beginning of the life by the Spirit. Knowing the Holy Spirit will set you free from all bondage of the law, and into personal relationship.

Wherever the Holy Spirit is present, the power of the Lord is present. He will set you free from any bondage that has held your life.

What Difference Will the Holy Spirit Make?

'You shall receive power.' (Acts 1:8)

Do you want power? Power to preach the gospel, power to heal the sick, power to cast out demons?

If the answer is 'Yes', then you need to know the Holy Spirit. Don't just seek his power for if you do, you'll miss the best. Seek his friendship, and the power will flow naturally from the relationship that you have with him. If you are daily talking with the Holy Spirit then surely whoever you come into contact with, is also going to sense his presence; that's when miracles happen.

I challenge you right now to say 'Holy Spirit can I really know you? I would like us to be friends.'

I pray that as you say that from the bottom of your heart, that today will be the start of a wonderful friendship with the most wonderful person that you can ever meet.

What Difference Will the Holy Spirit Make?

All the Difference!